Hear My Voice
And Come Home

Hear My Voice And Come Home

The Two Worlds We Live In

Marcus Foehner

Columbus, Ohio

The views and opinions expressed in this book are solely those of the author and do not reflect the views or opinions of Gatekeeper Press. Gatekeeper Press is not to be held responsible for and expressly disclaims responsibility of the content herein.

Hear My Voice And Come Home: The Two Worlds We Live In

Published by Gatekeeper Press
2167 Stringtown Rd, Suite 109
Columbus, OH 43123-2989
www.GatekeeperPress.com

Copyright © 2021 by Marcus Foehner
All rights reserved. Neither this book, nor any parts within it may be sold or reproduced in any form or by any electronic or mechanical means, including information storage and retrieval systems, without permission in writing from the author. The only exception is by a reviewer, who may quote short excerpts in a review.

The cover design, interior formatting, typesetting, and editorial work for this book are entirely the product of the author. Gatekeeper Press did not participate in and is not responsible for any aspect of these elements.

ISBN (paperback): 9781662912382
eISBN: 9781662912399

Contents

Preface   7

First Chapter
My Path   9

Second Chapter
Ancient Information   21

Third Chapter
The New Covenant   35

Fourth Chapter
The Two Worlds We Live In   45

Fifth Chapter
Reality   61

Sixth Chapter
The Change   79

Preface

This book came to me through a voice in my mind, like someone was talking to me but not through my ears. When I started writing down these words, they flowed out of me and onto the page from God. Jesus Christ is here among us in the form of the holy spirit. Preachers, ministers, pastors, and priests all point to a church building to be with him. I looked for him for years until I realized he was always with me and in the present moment. Before that, I couldn't find him, the kingdom of God, or peace.

First Chapter

My Path

As a kid, I never liked school. I hated being told what to do, when and where to do it, and who to do it with. I didn't know God and didn't care about pleasing him. I just didn't think about God that way. Eventually, I knew a little about God's rules. At times, I felt a kind of sense of them but still saw God as some guy in the sky. If one of his rules came between me and doing my will, I had nothing to do with that rule. I was into the physical world and lived worldly ways, apart from the Spirit. I broke all the rules that cause a separation from God's presence. I don't know if the chasm between God and me was larger when I broke more rules. If that was the case, we were apart from here to Pluto. I was doing my own thing, what, where, when, and with who I wanted to do it with.

Today, I can see that using drugs, (alcohol is a drug), made it easier to do my will and not God's will. But I didn't recognize it then. All I wanted was what I wanted, and if someone tried to tell me anything different, I left the scene. I didn't know it, but Satan had me out there in the world. We held hands and strolled through the world together, the world he rules.

I grew older, got married, was introduced to Christ, stopped using, got baptized, and had three children. My wife left me and took my babies with her. They were three years, one-and-a-half years, and six months old. Not knowing Christ well enough to lean on or to go to for help, I started using drugs, (alcohol is a drug), to kill the pain in my heart. So much anger, hurt, and fear was inside me, I did the only thing I knew. I reached outside of myself and into the world to kill the pain and help me cope. Drugs filled that huge hole in the center of my chest. My brain, the main frame, my CPU, knew how to solve the problem all right. Despite my limited information and resources, I received an email, ha, ha, ha. "Get high," was the message.

Twenty-seven years later, I lived out the consequences of that decision. After multiple in-patient, halfway house, outpatient programs, and self-help groups, I saw death coming at me like a freight train rushing down the tracks. That's when I knew I had to get straight, because that getting high was leading me to death.

One time after being released from in-patient, I started using again and thought to myself, *What's it going to take for me to stop this time?* It is a vicious cycle and is twice as hard to stop after starting up again. When I stopped for a while, I went to church and lived a full, free life, free from the chains of addiction. I heard bits and pieces about getting free and being free through Jesus Christ. I wanted to know Christ so we could become friends and walk together but didn't know how to do that. Each time, I heard or understood only enough to keep me hanging in there until I went back to active addiction.

Eviction and homelessness came into view, which were more train wrecks, and I knew I had to stop. I started going to two churches, one for Worship and one for Mass, five times a week. Finally, I listened with my heart and learned that God could break the chains and pull me out of bondage. In between church services, I hung out with the outreach minister, secretary, and pastor, where I continued to hear the message, the good news. They talked about freedom from bondage and a different lifestyle. I got involved with service work, which also kept me at church and focused on other people beside myself.

Before starting my day, I read the Bible every morning and prayed for help in understanding the Word. When I had questions about God or how to react as problems arose, I called fellow believers. The only way I could stay away from active addiction was to practice this new lifestyle.

As I mentioned earlier, it's always more difficult to stop using and stay stopped without starting again. A user who realizes he's an addict in his 20s doesn't have to change much of his life around to stop, to break the chains of addiction. A younger user hasn't spent many years living the lifestyle that addiction brings. Using isn't as ingrained in his thinking, actions, and behaviors as it is with someone who has lived that addiction lifestyle for 30 years. My change had to go deep, real deep, for me to get back on track.

As an example, I knew my way of solving and coping with feelings from conflicts didn't work too well. So I learned a new way to walk. Part of this change involved shifting my focus from myself and the carnal world to a focus on the idea of a selfless, Christ spirit. In my new lifestyle, I learned to walk with Jesus Messiah Christ, the King, and call myself a Christian. As a Christian, I needed to act and behave like someone living that lifestyle change. The people around me, especially those of the world and those who knew me, needed to see something different about me.

I began to worship God with all my heart, mind, spirit, soul, and voice. At first, I had a hard time remembering to pray, for I never really did. So I prayed for wisdom and knowledge to understand his Word, the Bible, Scripture. Five years after beginning this change, I began having strange thoughts and ideas. They kept coming to me. During the five years, I had these urges to write. And I did, like journaling little bits and pieces at a time, and it made me feel so good. I was at peace with who I was, where I was in my life, and everything that I owned. Total contentment.

After five years, the thoughts and ideas started. One evening a month later I walked into my dwelling and stepped onto the back deck, which was two steps up. Just before my foot touched the deck, a strong thought entered my mind, almost like hearing a voice but not through my ears but deep in my mind, this voice told me to get a pen and paper and sit and write. When I entered my house, I got busy doing something very meaningless and forgot. The next evening I walked into my dwelling place and stepped onto the back deck. I walked up the two steps and, just before my foot touched the deck, the same thoughts and voice came into my mind. I remember exactly where I was and what I was doing when the Spirit came upon me. Very strange, indeed. That time I grabbed a note pad, pen, and chair. Five pages later, front and back, I put the pen down, leaned back in my chair and thought, *What just happened? Where did that come from?* I shared those pages with a couple of people and what they meant. They said, "You are unique. You should write a book."

I called my mom and told her what happened and read her what came to me on those five pages. Mom said, "Where did that come from? That's not you." After a couple of calls where we talked about it, Mom said, "Stop, you're scaring me." Mom was baptized but didn't attend church regularly as an adult.

Well, I decided to write a book; this one. I've spent many years praying to do God's will, for God to use this body to do his will on earth. That's what is happening. People see and recognize only a small part of light and sound. Certain experiences such as being extremely tired, living a certain lifestyle, and changes in brain chemistry, including mental illness, allow someone to smell, taste, see, hear, and think of things that people who haven't experienced those situations don't see or experience. As I look back, I see where God was moving in my life for the things that I have lived through. Without his hand on me, I would be dead. I needed him then, and I need him now.

Like a seagull lost in the desert, I was out of place, trying to get back home. I was the same during my lifestyle change. I had to accept the light as the truth and seeing the dark as a lie, getting used to the light and not living in the dark. It was like two different worlds, before and after. I needed someone or something to guide me home. But I thought that God left me, because God didn't protect me from using, I believed that God didn't keep his promise when I fell into deeper addiction. This created a chasm between God and me. What I learned was that God gave me a choice. He didn't leave me, I left him. I created my own hell, and I was stuck in that place, that state of mind. Because I focused on the world instead of on God, I became familiar with hopelessness, despair, doubt, fear, loneliness, separation, depression, and anxiety. This created a separation and disconnected me from everything and everyone. As a consequence of reaching into the world for physical things to fill the hole in my chest, I had a disease, a disease. I trapped myself in insanity and unreality. The consequences were awful.

One of the consequences was jail. To me, jail was a safe house, a cake walk compared to the bone-grinding, teeth-gnashing way I lived in society and followed the ways of the world. When I was in jail, I felt safe from committing suicide or homicide as a result of my user lifestyle. I was safe from self.

I didn't like to look in the mirror, because I didn't like who I saw. After many months, when I did look, I wouldn't make eye contact. I was living out hell on earth. I was spiritually bankrupt, in the dark and cold where ancient evil dwelled. When you're lost in the woods for 27 miles, or years, it takes 27 miles, or years, to get back out. I was stuck.

One day I saw a piece of reality, a glimmer of light, a faint scent of hope coming from the destruction. The pieces, glimmers, and scents appeared, and then I slowly began knowing and believing that there was a better life. Knowing was half the battle. The other half was working on and living the change. It's like riding a bicycle up a steep hill. If I stopped peddling, I would slow down, stop moving forward, and start moving backward.

Through these slow and tiny glimpses, darkness was behind me, and the light was in front of me. I finally understood that if I'm not moving toward the light, I'm moving toward the darkness. Going back to the bicycle and the steep hill, I still had to peddle. And that was okay, because this new lifestyle was well worth it. Through Jesus Messiah Christ and the new covenant, the hills were not steep. Going to the light was a spiritual place in my mind through my thoughts. It was not a physical place like a church building, your hometown, or even your home itself. Ask a war veteran.

Hey, you never know. You never can tell. It only takes a split second to change your life to the good or the bad.

I am an overcomer.

The vices of the world, they had me bound tight. They hold me no more

Although they come to me, likes it's fun, and I want to do them again. Temptation is strong, and my flesh is weak

Self-centered pride and selfish ego start to rise

Sin looks okay, and it seems like God isn't around.

But Satan is a liar, and I rebuke Satan in the name of Jesus Christ. Oh, but I am a new creation in Christ, a child of God.

I do not want to sin. I am an overcomer.

Submitting to the fact, I do not need that in my life any more. I am an overcomer.

By Marcus Foehner

Second Chapter

Ancient Information

In Genesis, at the beginning of the Bible, God is the creator of everything, creating everything seen and unseen. God spoke the words and creation came into existence.

We are part of his creation. He created both man and woman and called them Adam and Eve. After creating a place for them to live, the Garden of Eden, and placing them there, God came and walked with them at the breezy time of the day. They doubted God, which caused separation between God and man. This separation is sin.

Eve bore two sons, and one killed the other. So the first four people lived and started the world. But one killed his brother. Humanity only got worse and turned bad and corrupt. God got fed up with mankind and flooded the earth to clean the corruption man created. He saved only Noah and his family and started over with mankind. God formed a community of people he called his own, the Hebrews. When they get one or two million strong, they couldn't live among each other peacefully without killing, fighting, stealing, and having sex with each other. This was the wilderness of sin, when the self will run riot. God gave his people some instructions, the Ten Commandments, so they could live at peace and stay united with each other and him.

God calls everyone to him, but only some of his children hear his voice. Out of those who hear him came the few who do his will. Even today, God is calling us. Do you hear his voice?

God spoke these words as instructions, called the Ten Commandments. These Scriptures are Deuteronomy 5: 7-21 from the New International Version N.I.V. quest study bible, published by Zondervan, copy write 1994, 2003, 2011, of the Holy Bible.

1. 'You shall have no other gods before me.

2. 'You shall not make for yourself a carved image—any likeness of anything that is in heaven above, or that is in the earth beneath, or that is in the water under the earth; you shall not bow down to them nor serve them. For I, the Lord your God, am a jealous God, visiting the iniquity of the fathers upon the children to the third and fourth generations of those who hate Me, but showing mercy to thousands, to those who love Me and keep My commandments.

3. 'You shall not take the name of the Lord your God in vain, for the Lord will not hold him guiltless who takes His name in vain.

4. 'Observe the Sabbath day, to keep it holy, as the Lord your God commanded you. Six days you shall labor and do all your work, but the seventh day is the Sabbath of the Lord your God. In it you shall do no work: you, nor your son, nor your daughter, nor your male servant, nor your female servant, nor your ox, nor your donkey, nor any of your cattle,

nor your stranger who is within your gates, that your male servant and your female servant may rest as well as you. And remember that you were a slave in the land of Egypt, and the Lord your God brought you out from there by a mighty hand and by an outstretched arm; therefore the Lord your God commanded you to keep the Sabbath day.

5. 'Honor your father and your mother, as the Lord your God has commanded you, that your days may be long, and that it may be well with you in the land which the Lord your God is giving you.

6. 'You shall not murder.

7. 'You shall not commit adultery.

8. 'You shall not steal.

9. 'You shall not bear false witness against your neighbor.

10. 'You shall not covet your neighbor's wife; and you shall not desire your neighbor's house, his field, his male servant, his

> female servant, his ox, his donkey, or anything that is your neighbor's.'

Exodus = a mass departure.

Commandment = a rule that must be obeyed.

Covenant = an agreement between God and his people, in which God makes promises to his people and, usually, requires certain conduct from them.

Contract = a written or spoken agreement between two parties where specific duties are to be performed.

Relationship = the way in which two or more people or things are connected, or the state of being connected.

Instructions = 1. The act of teaching or informing the understanding in that of which it was before ignorant; information. 2. Precepts conveying knowledge. 3. Direction; order; command; mandate.

Love is the way. As a parent loves their children, so God the Father loves us, his children. In a marriage relationship, a husband and wife are connected though an agreement of vows and commitments. We are obedient to the stipulations in the vows we agreed to, which strengthens the relationship between both parties and helps them live in peace. The bride and groom agreed to enter into a contract, or covenant, between each other.

My relationship with God is very similar. Obeying the rules and instructions keeps me united with God, which is good. Disobeying these rules or breaking the covenant separates me from God, which is bad. When I disobey God, this causes a separation between God and me. This separation is sin. But God said that if a man builds an altar, sacrifices a live animal, sheds blood on it for the time the man disobeyed him, God will forgive the man so they may be reunited.

Somehow, we humans messed that up, and we were separated from God, which is bad. The animal sacrifice stopped working. The scribes and Pharisees and such who performed the job God assigned to them turned selfish and self-cen-tered. This caused a separation between the people and God by driving a wedge, when these scribes and Pharisees were supposed to remove the separation and unite people with God.

Peace with God is the most important rule to follow, for without God there is no peace. God wants to have a relationship with his chosen people and live among them on the condition that they follow the rules he gave them to live in peace. It's like man couldn't figure out how to achieve and maintain a peaceful life united with God and each other. Breaking the rules separated them from God. Well, the community did it again, and corruption and separation from God came back.

I heard that God gathered all the angels and saints together and wondered how to get the people reunited with him. Satan, a fallen angel, said, "I can do it. I can reunite you and your people."

God said, "Not a chance, Devil. I'll do it. I'll reunite my people back to me." God decided to come down on earth, walk in the dirt he created, and literally show humankind how to do it. God drew the blueprints and laid the foundation to having peace and unity with God and one another.

Sin = the separation from God.

Atonement = being reconciled, trading sins for sacrifices.

Alter = God's table. a sacred place for sacrifices and gifts offered up to God.

Sacrifice = an act of slaughtering an animal or surrendering a possession as an offering to God.

Salvation = the act of saving someone from sin or evil. Deliverance from the power and effects of sin.

Salvation through Jesus Christ keeps me in Gods presence, and that happens at the altar. So, God came to earth, took on skin, and walked among us as Jesus

Christ, the Son of God. Yes, God's one and

only son. I was confused about it when I first heard that God came and took on flesh and was called the Son of God. You see, God has many names.

Along came this guy named Jesus. He told the religious leaders he was the Son of God, the Messiah they waited for, the one who was written in their scriptures of the Old Testament. Jesus told the Jews the truth about the scriptures being fulfilled right before their eyes and said that they were off target, that they were wrong. They not only missed the bullseye, they missed the target.

God created everything and is part of everything and is everywhere. This makes everything good, because God is good all the time, and all the time God is good. He brought life to creation in and of himself and gave everything life from him. He is life.

In the Gospel according to Saint John, God came to John and took John back to the beginning of creation. John wrote about who Jesus is in chapter 1 verses 1-14, are from the New Living Translation of the Holy Bible.

1. In the beginning the Word already existed. The Word was with God, and the Word was God.

2. He existed in the beginning with God.

3. God created everything through him, and nothing was created except through him.

4. The Word gave life to everything that was created, and his life brought light to everyone.

5. The light shines in the darkness, and the darkness can never extinguish it.

6. God sent a man, John the Baptist.

7. To tell about the light so that everyone might believe because of his testimony.

8. John himself was not the light; he was simply a witness to tell about the light.

9. The one who is the true light, who gives light to everyone, was coming into the world.

10. He came into the very world he created, but the world didn't recognize him.

11. He came to his own people, and even they rejected him.

12. But to all who believed him and accepted him, he gave the right to become children of God.

13. They are reborn—not with a physical birth resulting from human passion or plan, but a birth that comes from God.

14. So the Word became human and made his home among us. He was full of unfailing love and faithfulness. And we have seen his glory, the glory of the Father's one and only Son (The Holy Bible, the new living translation, Tyndale House Publishers, Inc.).

The Word

Word = a single distinct meaningful element of speech or writing; an element of speech or writing.

Element = a part or aspect of something abstract, especially one that is essential or characteristic abstract; existing in thought or as an idea but not having a physical or concrete existence.

Essential = constituting or being a part of the nature or essence of something, absolutely necessary, indispensable, -characteristic= a distinguishing trait, quality, or property.

Aspect = a particular status or phase in which something appears or may be regarded.

So word must mean a single distinct meaningful particular status or phase in which something appears or may be regarded existing in thought or as an idea but not having physical or concrete existence, especially one that is absolutely necessary or having a distinguishing trait, quality, or property. It can be something floating in space, in one's mind. Not being a part of the mind but as a cloud coming in, passing thru, and going out of the atmosphere of the mind.

Thought

Thought = the act or process of thinking. A judgement, opinion, or belief.

Eternal = without beginning or end / always existing / everlasting or universal spirit, as represented by God.

Law = instructions.

Eternal thought = thought is the Word, the Word is the act, and action comes from the Word.

Eternal law = eternal thought, word, act. Law is with God and goes before God, from God. Law created everything, and without it there was nothing.

Mind = a place to think / minds nature is act of thinking.

Third Chapter

The New Covenant

The new covenant is Jesus Messiah Christ. He is the final blood sacrifice, a human crucified alongside the road. He died, was buried, and finally rose out of the grave into the kingdom of God. But Jesus left his spirit with us to reunite us with God the Father, our Heavenly Father. As stated in John 1 earlier in this book, now that his spirit was everywhere around us and in us, Jesus Messiah Christ ushered in a new world and concepts to live. This was similar to what God did in the desert with the Hebrews, in Deuteronomy Chapter 5. He brought humankind a new way to live, think, act, and behave through new information, making a new contract, agreement, and stipulations between God and man so we could be reunited and have a relationship once again.

Jesus Messiah Christ was the final blood sacrifice and replaced the animal sacrifices. He took our wrongs, our dirty deeds, and our sins and erased them. How does this happen? When we confess these things to God, repent, and are sorry for not doing what God told us to do, I ask Jesus to forgive me, thank him for his forgiveness, then go right into praising him. Jesus Messiah Christ and I fulfil the obligations and stipulations that both parties agreed upon in the contract in exchange for specific services offered to the other. This happens at the alter in the temple. The alter is my mind, and the temple is my body.

When Jesus was totally unselfish and gave up his life while he hung on the cross, his spirit poured over all of creation. His spirit carried mercy, grace, and forgiveness. This reconnected us with God so that he became our Heavenly Father and we were connected in spirit. God sends us to Jesus and, after cleansing, Jesus sends us back to God.

We humans are born into his spirit and don't even know it. God is all around us, God is in us. The kingdom of God is all around us, the kingdom of God is in us. When God came to earth, he brought a new world. He hid himself, the new world, and the kingdom of God in plain sight, right among us. The world Jesus came into didn't recognize him or the new world he brought that made the two worlds where we live. The new world is an internal change in us. Believers become a new person when they walk in the spirit, believe in the new covenant with Jesus, have faith and trust in him. The old world doesn't recognize the new world Jesus created, as the world doesn't recognize Jesus. You can't be in both worlds, the old and new, the past, future, and the present, at the same time. If any of the old world is in the new, the new world becomes the old world.

The alter

The Hebrew alter was an old world piece of furniture where blood sacrifices took place to remove our sin. This was in the time before Jesus Messiah Christ was born, during the old covenant or old world. The alter was housed in a manmade structure called the temple. As mentioned previously in this book, the old covenant stated that when a man broke one of God's rules, he had to slaughter an animal on the alter for forgiveness to be cleansed of sin. The animal sacrifices were taken for granted. The old covenant agreement stopped working, and the cleansing couldn't take place to reunite God and man together again. The new world Christian alter is our mind. Under the new covenant, the cleansing takes place in our mind. The cleansing is housed in a different kind of holy temple, our body. This means that Jesus dwells in our body.

For me, cloudy thoughts trap me in a deceptive, fake reality that tells me it is the accurate reality. This fake reality tries to convince me that the truly accurate reality observed by other people does not exist. These cloudy thoughts and fake reality cause a separation that disconnects me from God. In other words, I sin. But God is good, and I notice the fake reality caused by the cloudy thoughts. I take those cloudy thoughts, the fake reality, to the alter in my mind. I go to the alter and clear and clean the cloudy thoughts I made from judging experiences and believing they are an accurate reality. I release my past and future and give everything to Christ. Then I humble myself in front of my Creator and give him my will and my life. I give him all of me.

Why do I give myself to God? Because I want a life without drugs and alcohol. So God needs less of me in the temple of my body and more of him in the temple. God wants the temple so empty that it echoes like an empty warehouse building. When there's so little of me, then Christ the King enters and fills up all of the empty spaces with his presence. With Christ in the temple, I have joy unstoppable.

So I climb on the alter and ask God to clear the cloudy thoughts.

I ask God to release my past, the experiences I created and the feelings that were created from believing the cloudy thoughts were an accurate reality. And God releases them. I ask God to remove the cloudy thoughts that caused me to live a worldly lifestyle, hurt people, kill things, tell lies, and fornicate. God sees the hate I allowed to flow out of me when I lived a worldly life, the disrespect I showed toward my parents, elders, and peers. When I lived a worldly lifestyle I put things before God that might be considered an act of adultery against him. I was angry with God, and I invoked his name in vain. When I lived a worldly lifestyle I stole and was jealous over the possessions of others and wanted those things. Of course, I could add more actions and behaviors. But God releases me from all of this.

I learned not just to confess but realized I must make some changes in my life. So I prayed that God would help me work out a solution so it would not happen again. I asked God to help me recognize the cloudy thoughts and stop judging experiences in the past. Dear Lord, I am so sorry and regret what I did against the one who loved me the most. God knew I felt shame, regret, remorse, and fear. He knew I was really sorry and feeling it. I asked Jesus Messiah Christ to forgive me, and through faith believed I received what I requested. Then I finish by thanking him for his forgiveness, mercy, and love. Jesus pulls me off the alter, wipes my mind clean, and places me in God's presence, in an accurate reality.

As I leave the alter, I know I am a child of God. This makes him my heavenly Father, and I have his divine power in me. Yes, I have God in me. That is where my alter, my mind, and my God are located. Jesus is the alter before you get to it, while approaching it, as you enter into it, and when you climb on top of it. When Jesus is the sacrifice and I give him all of myself, he does not cater to the flesh. When I leave the alter and finally walk away, I enter the Eternal Now, the kingdom of God, the Holy of Holies. I can only receive the Gift of Life when I'm in the present moment. Jesus is the gift that keeps giving, keeping us in God's presence.

The Holy of Holies must now be the mind in the body.

Jesus is the Word, and he created everything. Our minds are his creation. The mind is where thought begins in the vastness of space. Through thoughts, words, and acts, the mind drives our actions and behaviors. True thoughts, the thoughts of eternal law, put us in reality, in

God's presence, in the present moment, and in an eternal state of calm. For me, thinking about and judging my past experiences take me away from an accurate reality. This takes me out of God's presence into sin. The new covenant takes out cloudy thoughts or concerns about the past and future and takes us right into the present, in God's presence.

Thoughts to Ponder

New Covenant

New world

Temple

Alter

Holy of Holies

Sacrificial Lamb

Leaving the old world

Entering the new world

Starting a new life

Reunification

Change Renew

Kingdom of God

Creator

New beginning

Transform

Freedom

New creation in Christ

Resurrection

Spirit Separation

Jesus is the way, the truth, and the life. Pure thought and true reality.

Fourth Chapter

The Two Worlds We Live In

The old world is carnal and caters to the flesh. The new world is living in the spirit, in God's presence.

The old world — how humanity functioned while here on earth according to man's reality after generations, centuries, and millenniums from a corrupt thought process, resulting in thoughts and behaviors of greed, lust, pride, envy, gluttony, wrath, and sloth. Living for self.

Old — belonging only or chiefly to the past; former or previous.

World — human society or sophisticated society. The earth together with all of its countries, peoples, and natural features. A part or aspect of human life or of the natural features of the earth.

Greed — an inordinate or insatiable longing for material gain, be it food, money, status, or power. Wanting more and feeling sad and angry after losing material objects.

Lust — intense wanting for an object, or circumstance fulfilling the emotion, taking any form such as the lust for sexuality, money, or power, even mundane forms such as the lust for food as distinct from the need for food.

Pride — an inwardly directed emotion, a foolishly and irrationally corrupt sense of one's personal value, status, or accomplishments.

Envy — an emotion when a person lacks another's superior quality, achievement, or possession and either desires it or wishes that the other lacked it.

Gluttony — over-indulgence and over-consumption of food, drink, or wealth items. The excessive desire for food causes it to be withheld from the needy.

Wrath — an intense expression of emotion involving a strong, uncomfortable, and hostile response to a perceived action or speech that makes someone annoyed or angry, leading to hurt or threat, especially deliberately.

Sloth — without care. An affliction on a religious person causing them to be indifferent to their duties and obligations to God. Laziness, idleness.

Earlier in my life, I thought that God's ways weren't good enough. I refused to let God lead me, so I didn't follow his advice. Me, communicate with God? I sure didn't want to talk with him or learn from him through prayer. Instead, I believed in self-sufficiency and in living a separate life. All I wanted was to work and look out for myself. My world revolved around this "me" attitude. The physical world was all that was important. I lived a life of deceit, hate, and resentment. My life was full of judging people, places, and things. Because I was living in the world and not living in God, I saw lies as the truth and the truth as lies. I viewed unreal things as reality, and reality was viewed as unreal. My mind was closed off to new information, ideas, and thoughts. No way was I going to accept change. Why should I do something for someone else if I didn't get anything in return? I lived in fear of the past and the future. I didn't live in the present. Even now, that old world pulls at me and tries to get me back there out of and away from God, Jesus, the new covenant, and reality.

The new world — living for God. A new concept and thought process about living life on earth resulting in positive behaviors and consequences. It's getting out of the flesh and carnality and getting into the spirit, the Holy Spirit. Taking care of your neighbor's needs before yourself. Being content with what you have and have not. Thinking and acting through a Christ-centered, selfless mind, producing and promoting prudence, justice, temperance, courage, faith, hope, and charity. Living in the present moment away from past and future. Relying on God to lead our lives and to provide all our needs. God's presence is reality. Treat others as you want to be treated. Being open-minded and accepting change.

New — 1: not existing before: made, introduced, or discovered recently or now for the first time. 2: already existing but seen, experienced, or acquired recently or now for the first time.

Prudence — 1: the ability to govern and discipline oneself by the use of reason. 2: shrewdness in the management of affairs. 3: skill and good judgment in the use of resources. 4: caution or being wary and unwilling to take risks.

Justice — just behavior or treatment. Fairness, fair play, fair-mindedness, equity, evenhandedness, impartiality, objectivity, neutrality, honesty, righteousness, morals, morality. A concern for justice, peace, and genuine respect for people.

Temperance — moderation in action, thought, or feeling: restraint. Habitual moderation in the indulgence of the appetites or passions.

Courage — a stand for Biblical principles. The ability to do something that frightens you.

Being motivated from the heart to do something brave.

Faith — belief, trust, and loyalty to a person or thing. Finding security and hope in God as revealed in Jesus Christ. Saying yes to a relationship to God in the Holy Spirit through love and obedience as expressed in lives of discipleship and service. To feel secure. Acknowledging God in all our ways in contrast to relying on our own understanding. Confident trust based on God's promise as understood through his Word.

Hope — the confident expectation of what God has promised, and its strength is in His faithfulness.

Charity — the highest form of love, signifying the mutual love between God and man that is made manifest in unselfish love of one's fellow men.

God is in the present, where there is no beginning and no end. I am only with God in the present, for that is an accurate reality.

The present moment is a present from Christ that allows me to be in God's presence through the new covenant, the final blood sacrifice. Emanuel = God with us, God's presence creating the present moment all because of Jesus Messiah Christ. The present is God. Jesus Messiah Christ is "the gift." He's the gift to mankind, the greatest gift. Jesus is in the present moment, in God's presence, the kingdom of God, eternal. Peace. Love.

Past

Sometimes memories come and take me back to the past. The negative memories hurt and pull me away from God, out of the present. When I go to the past, I remember experiences and when I judge them they bring feelings and emotions that are positive or negative.

Is a newborn infant's first cry from pain? Or does the infant suffer discomfort from the recent memory of being warmed by the womb and wants it back? If I'm told a friend has just passed away, my face may drop and I'll say something like, "No way, you're joking."

If the response is, "No, your friend is gone," memories of the past flood my mind. Selfish self-centeredness enters, and I want my friend here with me. I miss them, and I won't share any more time with them. They are now a memory, they are now in the past. I can't physically go back to the past, only in memory. I could touch my friend in the present, but they are no longer here.

Next, feelings and emotions flood in, from the memories. These create a void in my life as I realize it will never be the same. Should have, would have, and could have thoughts cause feelings of hurt, regret, and anger. The undertaker isn't upset, he gets money. He has no memories of my friend. My friend didn't make him any memories. I cause my own pain and hurt while strolling down memory lane. I have to let go of my demands and expectations for how things should be. Hopefully, I soon realize that I can't look at what needs to be changed in the world, but what needs to be changed in me and my attitudes.

Present

God is good all the time, and all the time God is good. So why am I upset? Because I am thinking through a carnal, selfish viewpoint at the situation. It's how I see it. It is a mind game. But by controlling my thoughts to stay in the presence of God, it's easier to accept people, places, things, situations, and facts of life. When I do this, I am at peace and in the present. Nothing in God's world happens by mistake. I need to accept it as it is, only a memory from the past and not judge it. Being in God's presence brings peace and calm. Being in the past and future cause pain and suffering.

We are on a divine journey moving through time in God's creation. We go through seasons of change. Our bodies are born, we live, our body dies. We must notice it, not judge it, and move on. Rejecting it turns it into an issue, coming back to haunt us. Changes will affect places, people, and things. Bad things stick in my mind like Velcro®, and good things slide right through like Teflon™.

We have a natural birth that is physical, we live in the world, and then we experience a physical death. We have a spirit that we bring with us into creation, then leave creation and go into eternity. My spirit will never die.

While my body lives, I can't be selfish and also be in Christ. Selfishness brings memories, feelings, and emotions that cause me to forget about Christ and reality. Being in Christ brings Christ in me. This takes me into the kingdom of God, which brings the kingdom of God in me. A Christ mind is a selfless mind, never selfish. A Christ mind sees beyond feelings and emotions and is not affected by them. A Christ mind doesn't judge and sees that all things are good and part of God's plan, for he created them.

Am I a human being in a spiritual world or a spiritual being in a human world? I must stay Christ-centered, not self-centered, to stay in the present. I need to be free from feelings and emotions caused from my past or future. Maybe that's why dogs are so happy. They don't remember and can't go to the past. They are in God's presence in the present moment, having the gift all the time.

When I am weak, that's when God is at his strongest in me. God shows himself to me by showing me a way out when I am in the dark, suffering, at the bottom of the pit, being selfish and self-centered, not getting my way on how I see things should be, hopeless, at the end. I put myself deep, I mean way deep in the past out of the present moment. That creates a testimony; a revelation on realizing where I was, what it was like, what happened, and what it's like now.

Now I can talk about what freedom feels like. Being out of the past, future, and in the present confirms that a change took place. Remembering how it was pulls me from the present, and I learn from that to stay out of the past and future by not judging and just noticing thoughts that are unreal and false. The past is gone. From this moment forward, it's like waking up on Easter morning, also known as resurrection morning. It's quiet, fresh, pure reality. No thoughts of past or future create that freshness, that renewal. This is seeing the new covenant and being in the new world with Christ and the kingdom of God. It's an accurate reality.

You can cast your cares and your past and future judgments to Jesus through confession, repentance, and being sorry for your wrongs. Through prayer, you ask forgiveness for being separated from God. Then reconciliation ushers you into God's presence. That's where God is waiting for us to be reunited. It's like stomping my foot in a mud puddle and pushing all the water away from your shoe, if you have one on. The muddy water is all the baggage, issues, worries, doubts, thoughts, regrets, lies, fears, and expectations. It is the walls that are built up around you while traveling on earth, imprisoning you in the past. You create the separation all by yourself.

For me, when I'm in that present moment while all that stuff was pushed away, I was in pure and accurate reality. I caught a scent of fresh, clean, raw, new life in that moment. I found myself seeing and being the real me, not hiding or pretending to be someone else. I actually liked what and who I saw and who I was. In that moment, it felt so good to experience Jesus in the now, in the present moment. His presence in the present moment is a present, a gift. Holy macaroni, how many times do I have to repeat myself? God gave, and I received.

God is in me, and I am in God, experiencing his divine power in the present moment. Jesus said, "When you break a stick I am there, when you turn a stone, I am there. I am all around you, I am in you, the kingdom of God is all around you and the kingdom of God is in you." Why go to the past, away from God, out of the kingdom of God, when he is here with me in the present moment? He says, "Don't leave me by going there for I am here and that's all you need." I get 100 years, give or take, in God's creation as I'm walking, seeing, smelling, tasting, feeling, hearing, and thinking.

When I am pulled out of God's presence, I am unaware I was in Gods presence or leaving it. My selfish and self-centered thoughts about the past or future, whether good or bad, are a barrier between us. God has us going through time on a divine journey of his creation. The real issue is that I forget that. I created an issue. In reality, it isn't an issue, however. It's how I perceive a situation that brings on feelings. It's judging the experience.

God is good all the time, and all the time God is good. Therefore, the experience isn't bad or good, it just is. It is what it is. When an experience is created and I act on my beliefs by judging it, then it becomes an issue. That is how Satan gets me away from God and the spirit and leads me into the flesh, or sin. After giving my will and my life to God, I go my own way, doing my own thing. My beliefs lead me to judge, which makes me like or dislike something and clouds my thoughts. Clear thoughts are blocked, which creates distractions.

If I could keep my negative and positive beliefs out of my thoughts, I could remain neutral. We can get feelings when we judge the experiences. So instead of staying neutral, it becomes good or bad, pleasant or painful, liked or disliked. Judging pulls me from God and out of accurate reality. Having faith in Jesus, trusting and believing in Jesus Messiah Christ, allows him to lead and make my choices for me so I don't have to choose or judge. I can see things as they really are through pure thought and pure reality. Looking at the experience through Christ's eyes, with a Christ mind, I stay with

God. Christ is selfless, and I can't be in Christ and selfish at the same time. Christ doesn't move away from our union, I do. Inaccurate, and cloudy thoughts create the separation. So the issue occurs when I judge a memory of a past experience. I'm selfish, control, remembering how the experience should be to my expectations and beliefs, not Gods. That brings feelings and emotions, which cause me to lose sight of accurate reality. I forget that I'm on a divine journey.

- WHERE IS THE BEGINNING OF THE PAST?
- IS OUR BIRTH THE BEGINNING OR END OF THE PAST?
- WHERE IS THE END OF THE PAST?
- WHERE IS THE BEGINNING OF THE PRESENT?
- WHERE IS THE END OF THE PRESENT?
- WHERE IS THE BEGINNING OF THE FUTURE?
- DOES THE FUTURE HAVE AN END?
- IS DEATH THE BEGINNING OR END OF OUR FUTUTE?
- ARE WE ALWAYS ON THE INFINATE EDGE OF PAST, PRESENT, FUTURE?
- WHERE'S THAT CONFOUNDED BRIDGE?

Fifth Chapter

Reality

Jesus Messiah Christ is God in flesh, the son of God, the Light, Life, Creator, Creation, Energy. God spoke words that brought everything into existence. He created the earth and starting the beginning of the world. Jesus Messiah Christ created everything. He declared it good, and is in everything that he created, giving me a 100-year window in his creation. I know that I am in Jesus. Jesus is in me. Jesus is in God. And God is in Jesus. I am his holy temple, where he dwells. God is good all the time, and all the time God is good.

The present turns into the past when we remember an experience. The time it takes to change our thoughts can happen in a split second, almost faster than the speed of light. It ends when we think of an experience that we've made, as fast as we can think. So after that split second, memory kicks in and sends us to the past or future and thinking about an experience that occurred or will occure. This leads us to judge with a selfish, self-centered, fleshly, carnal mind and not with a selfless, Jesus mind. Having selfish and judgmental thoughts creates emotions and pulls me away from reality, out of my mind, out of the spirit and into the world. It causes me to forget that I'm traveling through God's creation and have the gift of life. The split second of the past happens after the split second of the present before the split second of the future, which continues a cycle forever.

I come from God and through Jesus Christ, I will go back to him. Jesus is the final blood sacrificethat brings me back to God. The true Gospel of Jesus Christ. Gods light, life, and energy became flesh, the same as me. He carried the same life, light, and energy in me. Living his will while in his creation. I know and believe that I am adopted by the heavenly Father, which makes me a child of God.

I am a human sacrifice when I'm living his will and not mine. He takes me out of the world, out of the physical and carnal world, and into his presences only by giving him complete control over my flesh and over my life surrendering everything to him. I realize I'm carrying God inside me and living in his creation, bringing his light, life, and even him into the physical and carnal world. His presence is in the present. The presence comes from God in spirit, goes to Jesus through the flesh in his creation, and goes back to God in spirit.

Surfing the eternal wave

Let's look at a surfer riding a wave on his surf board. The water behind his board is the past. The water under his board is the present. The water in front of his board is the future. For the rider to stay on his board, he must keep clear water under his board by choosing clear water that is in front of the board. If he's distracted and makes the wrong decision by looking at the water behind or the water too far in front, he goes into cloudy water. That's where the surfer falls off the board. He falls into the water behind the board, away from his board and the wave. For the surfer to get back on the wave, he has to swim to his board and climb back on the board. Then he has to paddle the board to the right place in the water and catch the right wave that puts clear water under his board. This is like letting go of the past. The cycle goes on. The wave has no use for time and has no beginning or end. It's an eternal wave. It keeps rolling and never separates from the water. The water creates the wave and allows the surfer on it. The surfer experiences time by being separate from the water.

The decisions I make in the present determine where I end up in the future. The path that I choose to take, the direction that I walk, from these choices I make they become the past. I live the consequences of my choices in the present. Splitting seconds in our thoughts and our mind can't comprehend that ability. It is outside the box. God's reality is revealed to his people a little at a time. This revelation is his reality.

Splitting seconds

Have you ever considered seconds in time? There are 1000 milliseconds in a second and one thousand microseconds in a millisecond. One million microseconds are in a second. One billion nanoseconds are in a second. Light travels at about 299,792,458 meters per second. Three nanoseconds is the speed of light. We think fast.

Jesus Messiah Christ takes my past, which is full of feelings and emotions, pleasant or painful. This helps me live in the present, in God's presence, in God, and be part of his reality and creation. It's also called a divine journey. When I cast all my cares and thoughts on Jesus Messiah Christ, I become part of that divine journey. I get to see the Word, to see life, to see God. Under the new covenant of the Gospel, our past, our selfishness, our self-centeredness go away. Issues go because they mean nothing. They are not part of God's plan or reality. As humans, we create the issue. And in reality, it is not an issue.

It is something that we experienced, how we see a situation we are in, or we were in, or we are about to be in.

God has the miracles, but he has no one to perform them. He needs a human sacrifice, someone like his son, to empty out themselves and bring God in. It's like using Moses to hit the rock to bring water from it. Come on, believers in Christ. Prove who you are and be the sacrifice. Or not. It's one or the other, and God will know. Have belief, faith, and trust in Jesus. Get in touch with the divine power inside of you and learn to communicate with it. Jesus shows you the way to emptying yourself and filling up with him. He shows you the way to live a simple life and bring out his divine power that's in each of us. Let your light shine.

- Reality
- Sacrifice
- Light
- Selflessness
- Spirit
- New Covenant

Baptism

New World

Believing

Faith

Trust

Change

Presence

Directions

Alter

Gospel

Life

Jesus Messiah Christ

Love

Spiritual

Sharing

Knowledge and Wisdom

Present Moment

Understanding

Jesus is in the Father, and the Father is in him. The Father is like the mind, it's reality. Jesus is like the thoughts in the mind. The Father in Jesus is like the feelings and emotions from pure thoughts. Jesus lived in, taught about, and spoke with others about the new world he brought with him. Being a living God he shared the Gospel, the good news that he is the way back to God, through the new covenant. The battle, the fight, and the front lines are in my thoughts. God is in my mind and gives me an accurate reality.

Experience causes thought and feelings that are not reality, however. Thoughts pass through my mind as clouds pass through the sky.

Clear thought is pure reality and in the present. Cloudy thoughts from past and future, is inaccurate reality or unreality. I can only be in an accurate reality and in the present with clear thoughts.

The new covenant takes away my past and future, which is the chasm that keeps me from God's presence. Jesus takes away my memories from past experiences when I broke or disobeyed

God's commands, laws, and instructions, leaving his presence. When I disobey, I judge myself. This creates cloudy thoughts that raises feelings, whether good or bad, that pull me into the sinful world. That creates another experience and the cycle continues, separating me from God until I go back to the alter and cast that experience of sin to Christ and seek love, mercy, and forgiveness. My belief, trust, and faith tell me that chasm is gone. Memories and thoughts of the experience are gone from my mind. I clear my cloudy thoughts of the lies and deceptions that are believing the lie that the experience is actual reality. Then I see it for what it is, false reality.

Satan is very close to eternal thoughts, particularly when my mind has a thought, which may lead to the Word, then goes into action. The fight is to keep the Word in my thoughts to play out God's will. Satan throws cloudy thoughts into my mind based on experiences and feelings. When I step away from the Word, I believe the cloudy thoughts are the actual truth, are reality. So we can't do God's will when we give the victory to Satan.

I lose the Word many times every day. Sometimes this happens from a lack of knowledge, wisdom, and understanding. I can't see actual reality because I get involved and distracted from pure and actual thoughts that keep me in pure and actual reality. This fight is a spiritual fight in the mind as thoughts drift through and I fight to stay in the present, in God, and alive. Separation from God causes death. But spiritual armor helps me win the spiritual fight to stay in the present, in Christ. Being at the alter keeps me in the present.

Satan wants control of the Word and the alter. He wants to pull me out of the present by tricking, deceiving, and lying about the Word with examples from the past. Satan may say something is pure and actual reality, the truth and convince me by dressing it up and making it look attractive. That makes me act on it, which takes me out of pure and actual reality and into the world. Remembering the experience pulls me into past or future. My judgment of the experience seals the deal, and I'm out of God's presence and into the carnal world from actions and behaviors.

Satan rules the world and can have his way with you when he gets you there and then act out on those feelings. It's a great battle between God and Satan to possess the Word. God is light, and Satan is darkness. Satan can never comprehend or put out the light. He can't get the power, the light. So what is he fighting for? It's the eternal battle of good against evil. Which kingdom will be the dominant force? The one who get the most people on their side to fight the spiritual battle for control of the Word. At the same time that God's people gather together as one, Satan's people also gather together as one. God's people live in the spirit, and Satan's people live in the flesh, carnality.

The kingdom of God, Jesus Christ, and the Holy Spirit is in the present. This kingdom is available to his chosen people through the crucifixion, death, and resurrection of Jesus Messiah Christ and believing Jesus Messiah Christ is the son of God clothed in flesh. Having faith and trust that when we live the way he said to, we will receive what he promised he would give us. Believing God came down to earth because he loves us and wants us to be with him, in his presence, in the present moment. Believing Jesus Messia Christ is The New Covenant, agreement, Contract. Give and receive by obeying the stipulations, rules, laws, and instructions. Giving of ourselves to receive the presence of God and being able to get in touch and use his Divinity, divine power that is in us. This is the good news, and believing it through water baptism is the Gospel. The past is Satan's playground, and it pulls us away from God. Do not go there, ever! It's Satan's trap. Instead, stay in Christ. God is shouting this through the Bible, the Gospel of Jesus messiah Christ, the good news, the Word became flesh. God almighty is telling us this.

The battle to stay in the present and the spiritual warfare are proof of Apostle Paul explaining what weapons we need to win this battle. Carnal flesh and Christ's spirit (Holy Spirit) fight for position. They fight for the possession of our thoughts, the Word. In the confines of my mind, it'sa battle between the past and the pure and actual present moments to direct my thoughts. Satan might be thinking, *How can I get him to believe me and act upon the thought I've created in his mind? It's a battle of flesh versus spirit.*

Try pointing to your mind. Where is your mind? The mind is between the brain and the soul. When a thought enters the mind, that thought is not reality. The mind is. God is reality. But what man thinks is reality and what is actual reality are very different.

In the present, Jesus has us in the palm of his hand and supplies all our needs. He also does this with the birds, but how much more are we than the birds? The birds are in the palm of Jesus' hand. That's where we need to be, by giving it all to Christ. Everything. We need to give our cares, worries, and problems to Christ. When we do that, it takes us into the pure and actual present with God, into perfection, in touch with and having understanding, knowledge and wisdom of being part of his creation. He is the creator, light, life, and energy. It must be none of me and all of him to get there in the pure and actual present. I must get out of God's way to allow his will to be done through me.

In emptying one's self to follow, I must let God lead. Self-sufficiency is a lie and a stumbling block. It's actually a road block forcing me to lead. That is me doing my will.

The problem is not the world, the problem is me. I am the problem. I think I know what is good for me, which is selfish. When I work with that idea, it creates a chasm between me and God. I should stop being carnal and selfish and let God do what he wants in my life, which is far greater than what I want in life. The devil deceives me in my thoughts, however, and sometimes I start doubting God's ability to take care of me. So I step into carnality and selfishness. I care for myself and take care of my needs as I see fit. I try to control life with my own understanding and judgement. But hopelessness is the result. I'm trapped in carnality and unable to get out.

Jesus gives me hope. His existence in me ushers me into spirit. "When you break a stick, I am there. When you turn, a stone I am there". Belief, Faith, and Trust. Totally believe who Jesus is. BELIEVING I must believe that he is Gods one and only beggoto son, the creator of everything seen and unseen. He is the new covenant that unites us with God. I must have supreme faith in him by living as he lived relying on him to take care of me and my needs. If I am in the pure and accurate presence of God, I will not need memory or don't need to remember anything. He has everything I need, so what else is there?

Humility is the perfect state of mind to enter the kingdom of God. It's difficult to stay in the pure and actual present moment with him, however. I return to the world and become part of the world, the old world, by becoming selfish and self-centered. I let my mind consider memories, feelings, and emotions. I'm no longer in God's presence, because I cater to my carnality and humanity. As humans, we don't comprehend the magnitude of Gods reality or being in the present moment with God. We are doomed when we use our own thinking and reasoning. We are selfish and self-centered. It is all for us. I, I, I. Me, me, me.

If we wore the cloak of selflessness like Jesus Messiah Christ, it would take us into his presence. We would not be separated from God. His presence is for his chosen, for those he calls.

It's for those who seek him and hear his voice, when he reveals himself to them. His presence is revealed to the humble who are doing his will according to the Gospel of Jesus Messiah Christ. It's for those who desire to live a spiritual life as he lived and teach what he taught for his kingdom, bringing the new world here on earth through the present moment here on earth.

You will be a free person when Jesus Messiah Christ comes into you. Through faith, belief, and trust, you will have the true experience of the Gospel of Jesus Messiah Christ. The new covenant will free you when you have a selfless mind that is driven by Christ. God unfolds the secrets of Scripture one spiritual principle at a time through his knowledge and wisdom. After you live one spiritual principle, knowledge, wisdom and understanding enter your thoughts, and you can work on the next spiritual principle. Each one is in order and leads to the next, in order, in the details. Then you will gain knowledge, wisdom, and understanding of the scriptures through practicing the spiritual principles that brought you that knowledge, wisdom, and understanding. This brings you a fuller understanding of the gospel of Jesus Messiah Christ. You will have a fuller understanding of the truth, the way, and the life you are supposed to live that brings you into the kingdom of God.

Spiritual principles are the things you can take with you to heaven. So let's push through all the distractions and learn them. You have to give them away to keep them. You give away what was given to you. Some people are afraid and embarrassed to share the good news, the spiritual principles they learned and don't want to talk about how God's knowledge, wisdom and understanding changed their life. They don't want to discuss how they found Christ or how the Gospel, Jesus, is alive, and living in them. Remember, "the word became flesh." Christ is the Word. God showed himself to us, but we do not share him. We don't allow his light to shine in the dark, and we deny Christ to the world. We don't show others the direction to get to God and live in the new world. We hide the lamp under a basket, and the lost can't see their way home.

Sixth Chapter

The Change

So let's look at living the change from the old world to the new world. Getting out of the flesh and into the spirit from darkness and death into light and life. We are to love our neighbor by practicing the corporal acts of mercy:

feed the hungry

give drink to the thirsty

invite strangers into your home clothe the naked

care for the sick visit the imprisoned

I live in the new covenant if I believe, have faith, trust Jesus Messiah Christ, and live the way he lived. Jesus' life was a blue print to being happy and content in the new world he brought with him. I should not be distracted by a worldly life. After all, I accepted a new way of life and practice that change. I need to be Christ-like and show people who are not believers how simple and peaceful life is by the way that I live. A picture paints a thousand words, so my actions and behaviors will show how to live a Christian life.

Christ lived in the new world, and God supplied all his needs. As Christ had no distractions, so he's told us not to be distracted. Jesus Christ places you in the palm of his hand, but he can't help you if you don't believe or have faith and trust in him. When you surrender yourself and live the new world life he brought and taught, he's got you. You're living the new covenant life in the new world he brought with him. Belief, faith, and trust are totally believing and living the way Jesus Christ lived and 6the way he told us to live in all your affairs, in everything you do, Allowing God to come through me brings the new world into being.

When I slip and think false reality is actual reality, I make life hard on myself and others. It's impossible to live the Gospel of Jesus Christ by living in the old ways, with the concepts I was taught in the old world. Jesus helps us change by introducing a new concept of living. One way is to sell everything and give the money to the poor because it is better to give than receive.

If I have a suit that doesn't fit, hanging in the closet, carnal, human, greedy thought says hold on to it. We are thinking in the flesh, thinking it's better to hold on to it, believing the lie as the truth. Our flesh and our thoughts reveal the way the world operates, how it deceives us.

That is not being Christ-minded. Christ said, "Sell everything you have and give the money to the poor." Christ also said it is easier for a camel to go through the eye of a needle than it is for a rich man to enter heaven. He spoke of the rich man living comfortably on earth and not getting into heaven because he has too many distractions that prevent him from doing God's will. As for me, I don't want to hear him say, "I never knew you."

Nearly 2,018 years later, that command has been tweaked, turned, justified, and rationalized. The world says it's a lie. Some Christians even say, "I don't have to do that." This principle has been twisted to please society and humanity. We're told we don't have to fulfill this command, a command which is good for us. But we see it as bad, which sucks us into being of the world, a world where Christ tries to pull us out of. Christ wants to keep us out of the physical, carnal, and fleshly world of mans wants and desires that battle within us, and have us remain in the spirit. Christ wants us to be content with what we have and what we don't have. God says that possessions are distractions that cause separation from him instead of living as Jesus lived and showing us the way to the kingdom. Jesus Messiah Christ teaches us how to live in the new world.

I believe that the early church strived to live in a Christian society. They wanted to live those command, those spiritual principle, so the society would be balanced. The early church believed that everyone had an equal net worth, particularly as they wanted to join together what man separated. They wanted to create peace on earth in a place where everyone's needs would be met. This would also eliminate the seven deadly sins; wrath, greed, sloth, pride, lust, envy, and gluttony. The early church believed that if they ushered in a peaceful, new world, a new way of thinking and living, that new life would fall into place. Everyone would filter their thoughts through a Christ-like mind. They wanted to have a selfless mind with selfless thoughts that put other people before themselves. They wanted to be people that God could work with.

The early Christians wanted to work for the same goal while living as one. That would make it easier to do God's will and live as Jesus Messiah Christ lived. The rich would want to give to the poor and only keep what they truly need to live on, thus making the poor rich. They would then have everything they needed to live on. The poor became rich, and the rich became poor. Then the "new" rich would give back to the "new" poor. This puts a balance in life and society closing the gap among rich and poor give everyone the same economic value. This practice got rid of the separation among rich and poor, in society, created a new world.

Today, God's true people get it. They understand this and live that life with knowledge, wisdom, and understanding believing Christ and divinity are in them. They have faith in what Christ promises and trust him by living as he commands. People of the world are not in touch with Christ or aware of the divinity in them. They live in sin and believe a false reality by keeping valuables and not living by this new Commandment.

Modern Christians show by their acts of mercy that they believe in an actual reality when they love their neighbor as they love themselves. Christ gave us this spiritual principal for life. People of the world live in a false reality that encourages pride, ego, greed, lust, and gluttony. These behaviors and actions keep the new world from growing as people rationalize and justify what's best for them. Christians who practice the unselfish ways of living that Christ commands remain in the pure and authentic present moment, in Gods reality.

The kingdom of God is all around you. The kingdom of God is in you. But a rich man has a very hard time getting into the kingdom if any at all. Earlier I mentioned the difficulty of passing a camel through the eye of a needle. One of the entrances into Jerusalem was called the Needle Gate. After the other gates were shut in the evening, visitors had to go through a very narrow gate to get inside the city walls. In order to get a camel through the gate, everything he was carrying had to be removed. Otherwise, the camel couldn't get through the gate.

It's similar for the kingdom of God. You can't get in with baggage. You can't enter the pure and present kingdom of God with baggage. Sell everything and give the money to the poor means you must get rid of the baggage. Fears of the future and regrets of the past are baggage. This baggage keeps us out of the present and separates us from God. We can enter with spiritual possessions we achived by the way we handled our physical possessions. Physical possessions bring regrets and fears that pull us out of the present away from the kingdom. We fight a fight that's not physical, but it's spiritual. We fight to stay in the presence of God, in the kingdom of God.

When I give all my cares to Christ, he wipes away my regrets of the past and fears of the future which are thoughts from memory after I think them. For example, as I am writing this book, my dog gets a cut on the tip of his ear. When he shakes his head, he throws blood drops everywhere. I want to put a bandage on it to contain the blood and to help the dog's ear to heal. So I put the pen down and bandage up his ear. The dog was a distraction that pulled me away from Gods will. I didn't keep in his Word. Christ is the Word that became flesh, but I didn't stay in him and keep writing. If I didn't have the dog as a distraction, as baggage, I would have kept writing and stayed in his Word, stayed in Christ, and kept on the path of doing God's will.

Here's another example. I get selfish and buy something that I want, like a new suit. I use money from my checking account for the purchase but I don't have extra money in my account. The money I used was suppose to help pay rent. "It" or "the want" is many things. I created separation from Christ through placing myself into the past and future. Soon I regret the purchase for fearing eviction. A simple man has few distractions. When someone is connected to the world, however, his wants, baggage, distractions, and complications pull him out of the present, away from God. He's not doing God's will, he's doing his will. Believing, having faith, and trusting in Christ allows me to get rid of my wants, my baggage, my distractions, and my complications. That is God's will, to stay with him and spread the gospel of Jesus Messiah Christ, to bring people into the new world and be united with him. With less baggage, it's easier to have less of me and more of God in my life.

Let's say I decide to watch a football game instead of spreading the Gospel. Did the apostle Paul play into the sports hype? He might have, but his leisure activities didn't make it into the Bible. Did they have leisure activities or distractions that pulled them away from God's will, from spreading the Gospel?

Jesus spoke about all of these things. The way he kept a simple life shows me the way, too. These things can either bring me into him or take me away from him. If someone is connected to the world with baggage and can't do God's will, they should get rid of it.

We have the Holy Spirit as a gift to help us and give us strength, wisdom, knowledge, and understanding to spread the Gospel through the new covenant. Faith, belief, and trust in Jesus Messiah Christ ushers in the Spirit and the gift of the Holy Spirit. You can take God, Jesus Messiah Christ, and the new covenant to the home of a Gentile. Through your testimony, you can tell them how the new life, new world concept changed the way you live. They may begin to do what they see, and soon a community is living and growing the new world.

Do possessions block you from total surrender? It's important to give all of yourself to God? Empty yourself by giving everything to Jesus. Allow God into your life by believing, having faith, and trusting that when you have no possessions, God will take care of you as you live that lifestyle.

Jesus saw Apostle Peter being the church by living the new world ways through believing, having faith, and trusting. An Apostolic Christian lives and teaches the new world Christ brought with him by living as Christ lived. This person is not deceived by believing that they need this thing or that thing to survive. Deception, selfishness, greed, lust, and gluttony are a reflection of our will, not God's will. This happens when we take control from God, which results in our sin. We do it to ourselves when we think we can do fine without God. It's a spiritual fight, not a physical fight.

God went to the poor and lowly, the people who lived simple lives and were not connected to the world with so many distractions, so much baggage. Apostles were called to leave everything they had and follow Christ. The apostles were told to go into the world with nothing and spread the good news. Huh, I wonder why? Actually, I don't wonder. I know why. With less baggage, they showed the way to the kingdom by example as Jesus Christ did and created the new world. It was a very simple life, although very difficult to live sometimes. Simple, not easy.

Pleasing the master

Solders in an army don't get caught up in civilian life. Doing so would break the rules and displease the superior officer who oversees them. The rules are for thier own good. Athletes can't win the prize without following the rules of there trainer and tournament. When they follow the rules, train, compete, and win, their coaches are pleased. A dog's total existence is to please his master. When the dog does what the master commands, the master is pleased. When we are obedient, do good, and please someone, we get praise from the person we pleased and are pleased. So it pleases God when we do good and be obedient to him. God wants us to be obedient by following his rules, laws, and commands which brings us peace. When we do these things, we stay connected to him. Our purpose is to please our master and creator. Disobeying God is not doing his will and what he wants us to do. A man that pleases God is a man after God's heart. A humble, simple boy named David did that and became a king.

God said to me, "I tell you over and over and over. I show you over and over and over again. You still don't get it. You slip into the past and future out of my presents by not obeying me. So I come down there, take on skin to walk on the earth that I created to physically, mentally and verbally showing you how to live.I'm the truth, way, and life. Hello. . . . THE WAY. . . I can't take you there only show you the way and then you have to find it on your own by following my instructions. Live as I lived. Doing what I did and not doing what I didn't do". Being a human sacrifice by giving up self and doing my Father's will. Doing that would have brought the new world and peace.

Moreover, of course, I was disobedient and did not do it so he had to come down here again and show us how to make it happen, peace on earth.

If you can't do it here on earth, you won't do it in heaven thus not entering or finding the kingdom of God."

The darkness cannot comprehend the light.

John 1:5 says, "The light shines in the darkness, And the darkness can never extinguish it." God is in the mind, in an internal space where he shines like the sun. Darkness doesn't recognize it is Jesus because it can't understand or comprehend him. It can't see him or recognize him, and darkness doesn't find this way to life. Darkness is being lost in the wilderness, not knowing reality, only experience, and part of the world.

I can't see the kingdom of God. I'm in the darkness. It's pitch black, dark, and I cannot see. I don't comprehend or understand what I cannot see. Events take place, I have so many distractions, how can I? The true light is reality. Experiences, what we experience, are not reality. They where physical and mental, not spiritual. When I'm in the spiritual place, I keep seeing the light, the truth, and the way.

Moses had the divine power in him to bring water out of a rock. People complained to Moses that they were thirsty, they wanted water to drink. Moses cries out to God and asked him what to do. God said to Moses that he should strike the rock and water would come out. Moses knew he had a connection with the God, divine power that was in him. Moses joined thought and emotion.

"Ask in my name according to my will and you shall receive." This type of asking is not done with a voice. The request is done with your mind and heart, through your heart, through the power of your heart. When I create the feeling in my heart as if my prayer has been answered, that creates energy that brings my answer.

Jesus Christ is the divine power and energy where life came from.

Remember John 1:4? "The word gave life to everything that was created, and his life brought light to everyone." So I feel as if my request has already been granted. I feel the feeling of receiving what I requested. I get surrounded by the feeling that what I desire is what I am praying for, the feeling of my request fulfilled, and enveloped by what I desire.

Ask without judgement and ask from the heart faith believing. To be means to feel as if by not judging. We have to put things in our hearts, not in our minds. I know I am connected to God, to divinity, to everything. Believing I have received it brings the feeling I received the gift, divinity. On the other hand, if I think I have not experienced this divine power, I believe that I am separate, alone, and a victim of circumstance. This creates my false image of self. That thought must be replaced with the truth of who and what I am and the power I have in me. I am a child of God, the temple that houses Jesus, the divine power.

This came to me and changed the path where I am walking. It showed me it has been a divine journey for the entire walk.

By Marcus Foehner

The world shows me pain every time I let it in. The world blocks me from doing God's will.

www.ingramcontent.com/pod-product-compliance
Lightning Source LLC
LaVergne TN
LVHW011731060526
838200LV00051B/3141